Jake is Stinky

Story by Charles J LaBelle
Illustration by Jake Stories Publishing

Jake Stories Publishing
Children's Stories and Jake Brain Training Games
www.jakestories.com

I0133043

Jake Stories Publishing
© 2016 Charles J LaBelle

All rights reserved.
No part of this work covered by the copyrights herein,
may be reproduced in any form or by any means,
graphic, electronic or mechanical,
without the prior written permission of the publisher.

National Library Archives of Canada Cataloguing in Publishing Data
LaBelle, Charles J.
Jake Stories Publishing
Jake is Stinky

Second revised Edition 2016
Illustration by Jake Stories Publishing
ISBN 978-1-896710-28-0

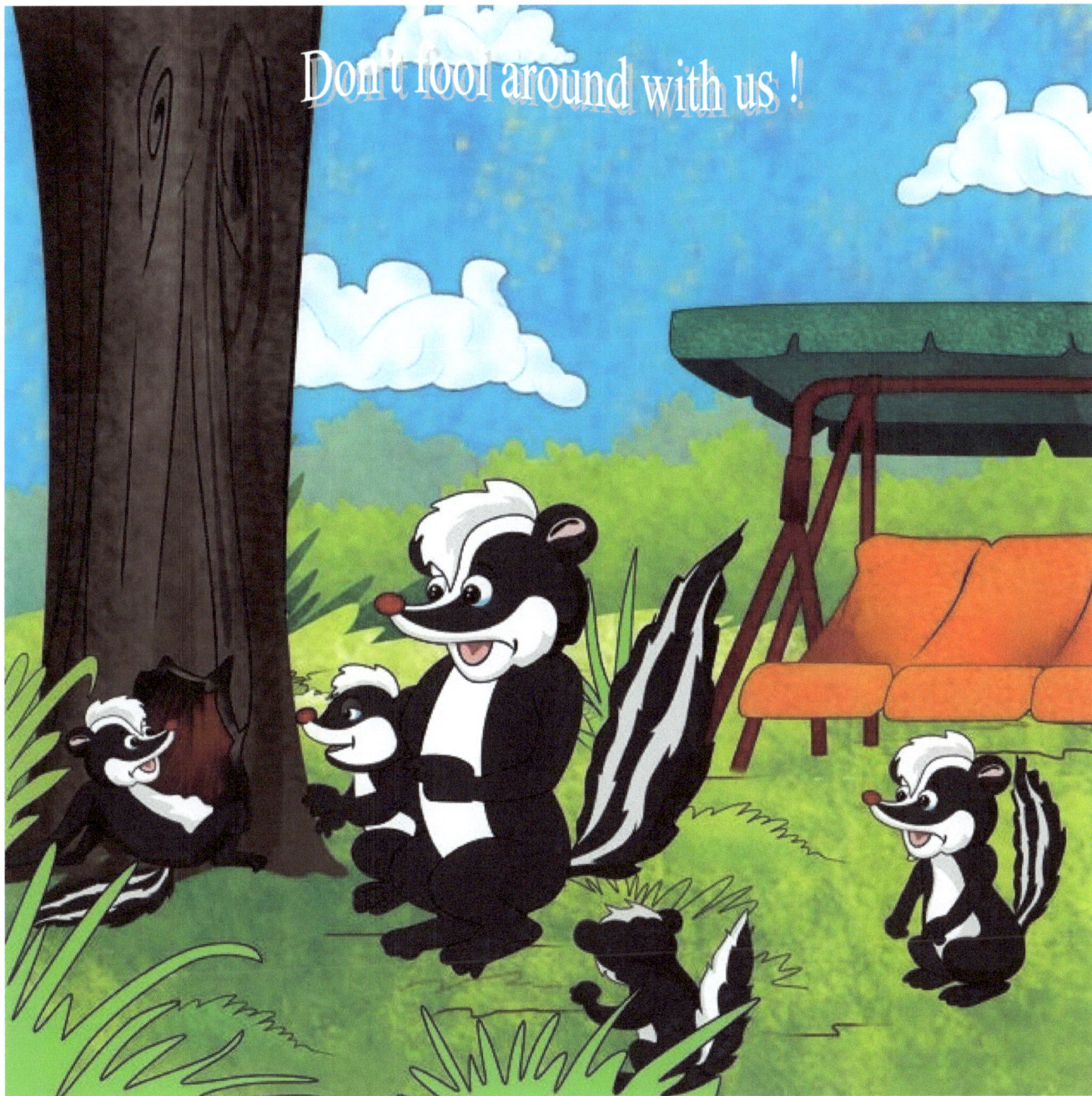

Don't fool around with us !!

A stinky breeze drifted through Jake's window.

Jake woke rubbing his nose and whispered,
"Piff piff, boom boom! Something smells funny."

He jumped out of bed, washed, and quickly dressed.

Jake thought,

Today I go to look for skunks with Peter. He knows a lot about animals.
He says skunks come out to look for food in the spring.

Jake crept downstairs into the kitchen to pack up some food.

He thought, *I don't want to wake Mom and Dad.*

He sang softly,
"♪♪ *Fruit, nuts and cheese should do the trick.*
If I eat healthy I won't get sick.
Good food for me and Peter too.
I'll bring enough to make a stew.
I'll take enough for breakfast and more for lunch.
And some popping corn for a bunch of skunks. ♪♪ "

Jake's Mom and Dad stuck their heads through the kitchen door.
They looked very sleepy.

Mom asked, **"Jake!** Where are you going so early in the morning?"

Dad asked, "Why do you have that big bag of food?"

"Piff piff, boom boom! Don't worry folks. I'll be back by noon,"
said Jake as he ran out the door.

Arf, Arf, Arf, said Arf.

Jake sang,
" ♫ *Arf can't come.*
He'll ruin the fun.
No dogs allowed.
I've got to run. ♫

Peter and I are going to have breakfast outside with some skunks."

Jake ran down the walk and turned towards Peter's house.

Dad asked, "Did he say skunks?"

"You must have heard wrong," said Mom.

Jake sang,
"♪♪ *Go down the block and over the hill.*
Climb on Peter's shed to the windowsill.
Don't make too much noise, just go knock! knock!
Wake up Peter.
Let's go for a walk. ♪♪ "

Peter rolled out of bed as Jake climbed in the window.
He asked, "What time is it?"

Jake answered, "It's six twenty-one and time to run."

Peter said, "**Wow!** I slept in. If you want to see skunks you have to get up early because they get up early."

Jake showed Peter the bag of food and said,
"Just get dressed. I packed us some breakfast and lunch and
popping corn for the skunks."

Peter asked as he got dressed,
"Wow! That's a lot. What did your Mom say?"

Jake replied,
"Mom and Dad were too sleepy to say a bunch
but Arf barked a lot when he saw the lunch."

Peter warned,
"Dogs and skunks don't mix."

Peter and Jake sang together as they climbed through the window.
"♫ *Climb over the sill and on the shed,*
then jump on the ground not the flower bed.
Run over the hill and down the block,
to McGregors' place where we play a lot,
where there are swings and tables, stinky skunks and rats,
and lots of fat old alley cats. ♫ "

When they reached the skunk's place Peter said,
"Put some popping corn near the stinky skunk hole.
Popping corn's what they like best.

Jake reached into his food bag, took out a handful of popping corn
and put it next to the hole in the ground that Peter showed him.

"Let's sit on the swing and wait. They'll come out soon," said Peter.

Jake sang,
"♪ *It's a four seater swing that rocks back and forth.*
Let's eat our breakfast with our backs to the north. ♪"

Jake and Peter sat in the old swing in the warm morning sun.
They ate their breakfast and waited for Motherstinky the skunk to
come out and eat the popping corn.

· · ·

They waited and they ate.
And then they ate and waited

· · ·

And then they fell asleep.

Motherstinky and her four babies came out of the skunk hole.
They looked at Jake and Peter asleep on the swing.
They sniffed the popping corn that Jake had left.

Motherstinky called,
"Hurry up, John and Jeri.
Chuck and Sue! You'd better hurry before the boys' wakeup.
Don't eat that popping corn now," said Motherstinky.
"The sun is too hot."
"I won't, Mom," said Sue.

"I won't, Mom," said Jeri.
"I won't Mom, said Chuck.
John asked, "Why not, Mom?"
Motherstinky answered,
"I'll tell you later.
Now come over here and eat the rest of this nice food the boys have
left on the swing."
The little skunks rushed over to the swing and helped Motherstinky
eat all that was left of the food.

As Motherstinky finished the last bite she noticed that John had eaten all the popping corn.
Now he was asleep in the sun.

Suddenly there was a loud sound and then another, then another.

POP! POP! POP!

John was bouncing off the ground with every pop.
His stomach got bigger and bigger.
His little belly was all bumpy looking.

Motherstinky ran back and forth, around and around.
She cried,
"Oh dear!
Oh dear! What can we do?
I told you not to eat the popping corn in the sun."

All the noise woke Jake and Peter up.

Jake said, "Wow! Look at all the skunks!
What's the matter with that little one?

Look! He's going, pop, pop, pop,
lying on his back with his legs up in the air."

Peter shouted,
"Look! His little bely is full of bumps!"

Arf! Arf! Arf!

said Arf.

Jake shouted! **"How did you get here?"**

"He snuck out to eat our lunch," said Peter.

Jake shouted,

"Oh no! He's chasing the skunks.

Watch out, Arf!"

Motherstinky shouted!

"Get back in the door hole."

The baby skunks ran down the skunk hole but John couldn't move because he was too full of popcorn.

Motherstinky squealed, growled, and spit.

She shouted,

"OK dog, you asked for it!"

She sprayed Arf,
Jake and Peter with a fine stinky spray that filled the air.

Arf cried,

Yelp !

Yelp !

Yelp !

He ran around in circles and rolled on the ground.

Jake grabbed Arf and held him tight.

Peter cried,
"Wow! Do we ever stink!
We better go home quick and get washed."

Jake gasped, wiped his face and said,
"Piff piff, boom boom!
We'll stink till June!
Now Mom won't let us in my room.

Cough cough! wheeze wheeze!
There's no wind now. Let's hope for a breeze."

Peter gasped,
"Arf stinks so much he makes me sick."

Peter shouted,
"That skunk spray makes Arf's coat real slick!"

Gasp ! Gasp !

Jake gasped and said,
"I hope we can get the stinky spray off.
Let's leave swings and tables, stinky skunks and rats,
and head for home like two scared cats."

Yelp ! Arf ! Cough !

They ran as fast as they could with Arf,
yelping, barking and coughing behind them.

Jake shouted!
"Let's find a place where we can get clean and put our clothes in a
washing machine."

The boys sang together,
" 🎵 *Let's go down the block and over the hill,*
jump off the ground and over the sill.🎵 "

They climbed up to Peter's bedroom window.

"Wait!"
said Peter's Dad.
"Not so fast!
Into the yard with the three of you."

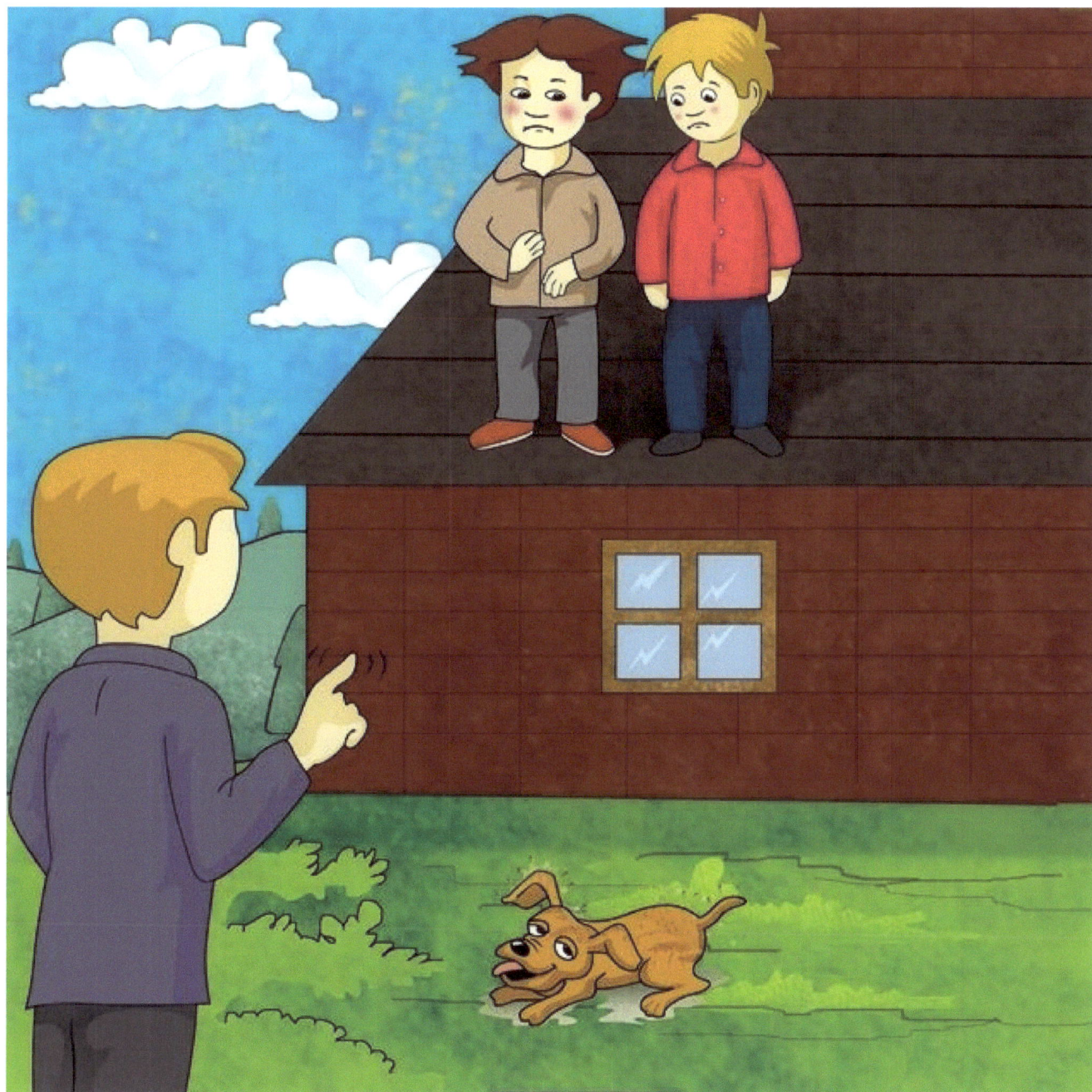

Peter's Dad instructed, "Peter, you get the hose.
Jake, you hold Arf and don't let him go."

Arf cried, **Yelp ! Yelp !**

Peter's Dad continued,
"Rub yourselves and Arf with this tomato juice.
Get under the hose, use lots of soap."

They all washed

. . .

they all washed and washed

. . .

and then they washed some more.

It was a good thing that it was a warm spring day.

While all this washing was going on,
Motherstinky was looking at baby John outside the skunk hole.

She said,
"My poor baby John. You're a mess.
Just look at you. You're twice your normal size and full of bumps."

John moaned. He said,
"I'll never eat popping corn in the sun again.
How long will it take me to be the same as I was before?"

Motherstinky answered,
"About four days if you stay out of the sun."

John cried, **"Oh no!"**

But he knew Mother was right, because she always was.

www.ingramcontent.com/pod-product-compliance
Lightning Source LLC
LaVergne TN
LVHW072109070426
835509LV00002B/82